INDISTINGUISHABLE FROM THE DARKNESS

POETRY

Red Roads

FICTION

Canaan

Shine Hawk

Indistinguishable from the DARKNESS

CHARLIE SMITH

W. W. NORTON & COMPANY · NEW YORK · LONDON

The text of this book is composed in Garamond.
Composition and manufacturing by the Maple-Vail Book Manufacturing Group.
Book design by Debra Morton Hoyt.

FIRST EDITION

Library of Congress Cataloging-in-Publication Data

Smith, Charlie, 1947–
    Indistinguishable from the darkness / Charlie Smith.—1st ed.
        p. cm.

    I. Title.
PS3569.M516315   1990
811'.54 — dc20   89–3307

ISBN 13: 978-0-393-30720-7

W. W. Norton & Company, Inc., 500 Fifth Avenue, New York, N.Y. 10110
W. W. Norton & Company Ltd., 37 Great Russell Street, London WC1B 3NU

1 2 3 4 5 6 7 8 9 0

Grateful acknowledgment is made to the editors of the following magazines
where some of these poems, occasionally in different versions, appeared: *American Poetry Review:* "Neither Ornamental Nor True," "Renewal: A Version."
Black Warrior Review: "American Drift," "Gosnold Pond" (winner BWR poetry
prize). *Chelsea:* "Ageling," "Sonnet," "Too Much, Never Enough," "Now I
Smack My Head." *Country Journal:* "Not Yet." *Crazyhorse:* "Heads of Fire,"
"Beauty Kills" ("In Virginia"), "Number Six Shot," "Testament of White,
Part Two: The Past." *Ironwood:* "Perception One," "On Evening Tide," "The
Meaning of Birds." *The Nation:* "The Holly Tree." *New Directions Anthology:*
"Slaughter Street," "Beauty Kills" ("In Virginia") (reprint), "Cycles" (reprint).
The New Yorker: "Indistinguishable from the Darkness." *North American Review:*
"Raison D'être." *The Paris Review:* "The Banquet," "Aquarium," "Cycles."
Shankpainter: "As in Japan This Morning." *Sonora Review:* "Kohaku," "Confederate States." *Southern Poetry Review:* "The Defiance of Heroes." *Southern
Review:* "Ex Regis."
"Beauty Kills" ("In Virginia") also was reprinted in the anthology *Poets for
Life: Seventy-Six Poets Respond to AIDS.*
To Stanley Kunitz, Mary Oliver, Tony Hoagland, Jill Bialosky, and Pam
Mandell, my heartfelt gratitude.

For Gretchen;
and for Moses Hoskins
and Gary Whittington
my friends

CONTENTS

ONE

TWO

THREE

FOUR

SKINS

These loose lyrics, too vague,
like the scattering of trees left over
from a cutting, so we can't tell
what forest, what nestlings
cowered there; and all day
the snakes crawl
between the water and me, and though I know
how beautiful they are, patterned
like an arrangement of gems, I wanted
instead a simple walk
across a plush green lawn,
and the pulling of oars . . . Though
all the while, even then, I see only a distance,
immanent and rarified,
skins of murky light.

—Jean-Luc Valois

Then why do your eyes hold an impure
gleam like the eyes of those who have not
tasted evil and long only for crime?
                                    —Milosz
                                "Slow River"

ONE

INDISTINGUISHABLE FROM THE DARKNESS

The dark under the trees is filled with lightning bugs
and because I am in one of those strange moods
I start to think I have found one of the hollows
where the life of the world is created. There is light
on the field still, a late light, bluish-gray, clear as water,
but in the dark circle of shadow under the oaks transformations
take place; small, accurate, invested points of light shiver
and rise wavering above the thin grass. I am in one of those moods
when I need this, this regenerative, tangibly formed
coinage, this dream or perception of the mixing vats
of the earth making out of nothing small light
that might continue to grow and change, become substantial.

The world of this field, sloping to a small black pond under trees,
is empty just now; on the side of the low mountain before me
the constructed lights of houses come on and shine like gold jackets
thrown up into the trees. It is spring and the breeze carries its mix
of summer and spring and the hint of dew that is not so much carried
as woven into the slippage of air; purplish clouds, thinned
nearly to haze, pile against the western rim. I have known
this mood before, and it comes sought but unbidden.
Like a shy child, it does not approach; the lightning bugs
do not translate themselves into negociable forms — a human
hand, the voice of a loved one. To become known
we must become unknown; the way out, I have learned,
is through. But I do not know
the names of the trees that are just now carefully laying
their long shadows across the body of the pond. The shadows
will lie on the surface of the water all night,
indistinguishable from darkness. It is not a matter
of being saved. I know this.

HEADS OF FIRE

Maybe you don't think pigeons
strutting along the sycamore limbs
mean much in a city of dangers, and the branches of elm,
weighted with rain, sagging
above the loitering police, are not necessary
to one who lingers at the edge
of a crowd, watching the most recent fire
step shyly from an eighth story window, but maybe you know
the black crease of smoke
from pretzels and souvlaki, and maybe
you have seen the chilled girl crying under the arch,
and maybe the man forcing a melody
from an unplugged guitar
has become essential; and maybe the broken knuckle
on your right hand is the only thing
keeping you from murder, and maybe
you have already been penetrated by everything
and are without defense
against aggression and love, and maybe
on a cold night in October, you too leaned a second
into the light to pull one away
who could never have hurt you, and took her
to a dark and abstract place,
and stripped her there of whatever was final
and most precious to her, and having had your way,
abandoned her — sated for a time —
and looking back down an alley of stone
saw her — just once, in a glance — sprawled
exhausted or destroyed across sticks of old lumber,
and noticed how the sweat and grease of her body

gleamed persuasively; and though later
you were not sorry, or even pensive,

you stopped for a moment by a fenced-in space
near the university, to look at a few ragged zinnias
spiraling out of weeds, and the sky,
back-lit, piled with clouds
that trembled like a troup of Bahamian acrobats,
seemed to pause for a second, or simply to stop;
and maybe you almost remembered what the last kind hand
felt like as it brushed a cake crumb from your wrist,
and your whole life almost turned for a moment,
the way Che, exhausted, having argued all night,
turned finally to his captors, and with an infinite
and heavy sorrow, opened his hands — as if, you thought,
as the zinnias nodded their heads of fire
at the stumbling wind, the moments of your life
were random couplings after all, vagrancies
detained for a moment then released,
not something else — otherwise —
as you had so often claimed,
as you had so often believed.

AQUARIUM

After the sporty dolphin show
you might wander down the dimmed aqua stairs
into a darkness they have cut windows
through, to see beyond the foggy glass
all fishes swimming. It's not a glass bowl,
but like the earth itself cut through,
so that you are a traveler
rising from the interior to this first glimpse
at the teeming world. They circle slowly: sharks,
jewfish, yellow fin; a stately manta pumps
its black wings, soars toward
the chopped surface, sinks into a turn, and disappears.
It is some kind of lion-with-the-lamb business,
all these varieties, cold killers and dumb
swimmers, schoolers, the lonely blue-throated
pilot fish, speckled distraught octopi
jammed under rocks. You have come out of sunlight
maybe, from the jaunty tricks
of trained porpoises who ring bells and
toss a ball and bark like crazy dogs, but down here
where it smells like the seabed, and your schooling neighbors
move shadily to grasp — as that man does — the
sills of small rectangular portals, holding
tightly as if onto the railing
above a gorge, and the slab side of a grouper
slides into view and you see the black incurious eye unblinking,
and the next,
and the light shafts down
to strike the hard back of a channel bass,
the cocked fin of a sawfish, you discover
another version of privacy in this voyeur's
den; like walking in on your father after the operation,
where as the black monitor ticks

6

its sad declarations you meet the gray dragged face,
the gray hand groping at the broken dorsal of his sex,
the gray, foolish smile he lifts and lets go
in the dust-stirred, murky room
that is like a tank you are both trapped in.

PERCEPTION ONE

What is already preposterous, the simple compilation
of unextraordinary detail — for example, three women
having coffee in a seaside restaurant as a brightly feathered bird
preens in a cage by the window — is not enough
to accommodate our lives this morning, is not exactly characteristic
of the emotional fever we have waken to. So the world

seems neither advent

nor explanation, and we are deflected, veer toward the south,
as perhaps the single phrase we traveled this great distance to hear
passes unremarked, and we look toward the waitress
thinking she must be the woman we saw dance
on a theater stage that afternoon in New York
when we passed the quivering purplous flowers
of wisteria heaped against the wrought-iron rail
enclosing a church on Twenty-First Street,
and thought how this was what we were supposed to discover in great
    cities:
a wall of flowers amid the steel, this
should settle and diminish our misery — but it didn't,
we raced on, fabulously fractured, amazed
that the obvious and persistent formula — perception into transfor-
    mation —
produced no results, did not even engage; so we ran on,
as something began to insist
that the world was more random than we thought,
that what we had gotten ourselves into this time
could not be appeased
or converted so simply,
that loss — or its mother, desire — would be a part of our lives now,

we would eat it as our daily bread.

AGELING

Involuntary religion
is everywhere today,
sliding down
like bird-flight upon us.
Across the valley farmers
call each other with bugles,
and the red-haired woman
saunters to the well
where in the fair egg-light of morning
she whispers to the day,
seeking gifts
to console her. I would like to live forever,

but free of responsibility; an ordinary thought.
I can't get over the lights swinging in the bay,

how dark the night is. There is no erosion in the stars,
the night is always black. This permanence

haunts me, dispels illusion
for good and all, so that in the sand under briars

I see the resolute rock, the stillness
that is the stillness of perpetuity; and the briars themselves,

twisted and spurred, repeating in aggregate
the same elaboration each year, mindless

and not defiant, like monks
praying lauds, will go on forever

as I will not. Already the flesh slackens,
a sullen sensuality

has settled in my face; my hands darken.

THE WHITE FACES

Each new moment — cruising along the salt pond,
the far dunes whitened to stone, splintered
sunlight — is not a new moment simply
because we have never seen this April
before, or because twenty million cells
have tugged themselves apart
and started over saying *That's a tree,
that's a burn scar, that's love,* or even because her red hair
never seemed so personal; nor is it
the memory of the year in Venice
when we held on through the winter rains
waiting for wisteria to blossom, and ate
raw crabs dipped in thin brown sauce, edgy
near the chemical water. It is not new
by extension, by repetition,
by accomplishment.

An indifferent porter moves through the car
plinking a small brass gong. This was years
ago. The white tablecloth, the leaded silverware,
the iris in a vase are rubbed
with immanence like works of art. The train
rattles out of woods
and runs for a few miles along a marshy bay.
Darkness has crept out to speak to the silver water.
You think you never saw such tenderness
as there is between land and sea tonight,
and you are surprised at the thought,
at the word *tenderness,* and then you see your face
painted from life
on the window pane, and it is nobody you know
in a car full of strange faces

like moody white flowers
nodding in the rain — the white faces
of cattle, stones in a field,
the blazing conjury of stars.

ON EVENING TIDE

At evening, as the tide comes in,
I walk downtown past festive men
who loiter in all manner of need
or appetite outside The Boathouse
clucking to each other, to the streaked
and bracing airs of summer night, to me
perhaps, or to the fact that I move, that I am alive
among the sprinklers bringing relief
to the lawns and the rugosa roses
shining like scarlet warning lights. I take myself
among them as another ambassador plenipotentiary,
one who knows something about the provinces
of the heart that are off limits, wondering, as I do,
about the arrangement of circumstance
and limitation that will prevent
communion, that will not even make an offer toward the moment
when each, turning to the other
among the sea oats, will take the unknowable,
unreachable form in his arms
and hold it, against pain, against the secret knowledge
of longing, against the imprecise
but relentless refusal — if refusal it is
(built like threads of steel into the frame of this planet) —
to be known . . .

I do not know why
we can love so hard
and so awkwardly, why now, under the shadow of locust trees,
the air has turned purple, and the streets —
which are simply returning from rain —
appear permanently stained,
why there is such a thing at all
as loneliness, why it is easy

among this precipitate crowd
to imagine someone, a woman perhaps,
standing alone at an upstairs bedroom window,
a woman who looks out on a gray lawn
swept with rain, on the mindless tossing
of pine trees, who herself imagines
that beyond the tops of the farthest trees
an ocean, gray as breath, stretches away,
like the sea of the Phoenecians,
who, arrived at the great gate of Gibraltor,
backed sail against the wind
and stared out, before they turned away, humbled
and terrified,
before indivisible mystery.

I am one who knows the scummy lake margins
and the call of upland birds;
I am one who has climbed all afternoon
through forests that retreated as I climbed
to come late in the day
upon a small battered house perched beside a spring,
and forced the lock
to find bed, table, and chair
all carefully arranged, cutlery in place,
the taut spread gone gray, oil clotted in the lamps . . . I am one
who lingered in the silence
not imagining the departed lodger
might yet call out, but that
the silence itself might become a form of speech,
the mastery of which might be a means
to hold all things — as perhaps it is,
as perhaps it does, the way
tonight, as the crowd of revelers

and true believers moves upon itself, beyond
any of us we could see, if we looked,
the flat, unimpeachable sea
from which the late sky drains
all substance — light
and form — save what we fling out on it,
sails or cries, flying forth into the dark.

WITHOUT HEAVEN

The lights pull the buildings upward
out of the park's dark drizzle, above
the glassy meadow and the cranky bodies
of the trees,
              so that, if you think this way,
there might be a space, a pavilion
of ghostly apparency between earth and sky, as of a lid
lifted off steaming cabbage;
                            and you now,
so frankly without recourse, having arrived,
at an age when most lives are sediment,
to a version that is less and less
explainable, and more and more
the only version, wish into being — and easily make —
in this space a phantasmagoria, not of heraldry
or heroics, but of a cudgling simplicity,
such as one might make out of a brocade vest
hanging from a branch, or of a white glove
floating on a pond —
                     and you hope that this,
like a hot cup of tea on a chill afternoon,
might turn your life around for a moment,
long enough for the simplicities
of birth and death, and the in-between, to begin to handle you
in a gentle way, like treasure.
                               But as you do this
you remember it is only a park
in a small city in the west, only wind
stepping gravely ashore, that the lights,
which are the residue of enterprise, of illicit
love and families,
will soon go out,

                    not struck out
by the hands of gods, but by cleaning women,
by businessmen stumbling to their beds after a trying day,
by a child who kneels in the dark by his window
to pray the one prayer he has learned,
speaking it carefully and firmly into the great world
he neither knows nor understands.

It is one of those moments, you think, when,
for a second, one loses heart.

SLAUGHTER STREET

One time years ago a man tried to sell
me a girl he claimed
was his daughter; with his thumbnail
he pushed the lank, loose hair away from her face,
he traced
with his forefinger the proposal
of her lips, the thin lifted
shills of her breasts. I think
I wanted to hit him, but I didn't.
I said yes, and took her away
under the mimosas that were wet with the afternoon's
rain, thinking that like a cat
I couldn't keep, I would set her loose
in the desert. But she wasn't a cat
and from that town it was miles
to the desert — we wound up, somehow,
on a street whose enamel gutters
ran in the mornings with the blood of slaughtered hogs,
drinking at the tin bar
of a dark place, where a three-piece band
played music compounded of gravel
and sarcasm, and women in ripped dresses
danced wildly, as if in torment, with thin men
who cracked pecans
between their teeth as they danced, and laughed
at nothing. I remember for one moment
I looked at her small face
and thought I saw my own romantic notion
of promise fall from it, but maybe
I didn't see anything at all, and maybe she had stopped
caring long before
I blundered by, but whatever I might have thought
I soon forgot — quickly, quickly — so that

when I looked again the gray dawn
was getting to its feet in the doorway,
and a man I had never seen before snored on top of the bar,
and the wild women
had retreated into the mossy places
they hid in during the day;
and she was gone, without blessing
or any enterprise I could muster, lost
to the claims of the street,
from which came now the squeals
of pigs, as the quick knives
opened the large vein in their throats,
and allowed
what they had been keeping to themselves
to pour forth.

EX REGIS

As the road narrows — though it does not
narrow — sinking from the black pine
woods downward into the dark tangle
of the river branch, I begin again
to make resolutions, thinking of Tolstoy's
ineffectual urban aristocrats, those failed
brothers and nobles, apoplectic and doomed,
ordering servants around. My life
is a tangled mystery again, and this
is not news, but only an amplification
of an earlier announcement. Down home

my brother sadly shows the slides
from Scotland, and I see on the hills of Skye
the half-dozen humans I am related to
by blood, sinking separately
into tall grass, each mesmerized
by some pointless, individual sorrow,
and though I did once I no longer
feel like comforting them. I don't know
if it is age, or the simple knowledge
that life is difficult, but it is not strange
to me now that a man will excuse himself
to go out into the little yard
where he sits for an hour
alone and mute trying to merge something
in himself with nothing. The sky

is an elaborate orchestration
of possibility, if possibility
were color and a structure
of light, which even now, on a mild

day in January, has made webs
and streams of pale, tremulous fire
out of the simple crowns
of conifers. And if I have married

again and started over, it is not
for the romantic notion
that a prize might be won at last,
or that an obstinate past, too long
endured, might finally
fade. I think of the early Roman kings
who in spring painted their faces red,
sewed gold leaves into their clothes,
and rode about the city
holding a brazen staff aloft. It was not,
I believe, the triumph of power
or the limits of ancient reason
that made the onlookers fall to their knees
to worship this, but simply the reverence
any citizen might show toward the ridiculous
and noble effort to transform suffering
into spectacle. Just so one might,

arriving at a small collection of cottages
partway through a long journey, step
wearily from the car to stand
a moment, perhaps arm in arm
with the one who is not so new after all,
but is, after all, a fellow — by right
of breath and proximity — communicant,
to watch, in a near field, the late breeze
make small, rippling pools of itself

in the pale grasses, and wish
into life — even see — painted kings
and their courtiers riding grandly
toward the dark, annihilating woods.

TWO

THE BANQUET

I went down to Missalonghi
with my oldest friend — this was a long time ago.
We visited Byron's house,
which is the color of bisquits
and smaller and shabbier than I imagined.
I thought of the way he let himself die,
how he just gave in to all the misery
he had caused himself
and it was meaningless
to me I was agitated,
falling out of love with my friend
who was my lover
and the lover of the woman who had left me
the year before. We stopped at a restaurant on the highway
and stood a moment looking at the tan-and-yellow
shabby grasses blowing
on the hillside. They looked as if they were heading
somewhere, toward at least
the gray olive trees among the rocks. Inside
a squat man, still young, led us from our table
to a banquet of dishes
laid out on a counter, pointing out the fish
and the wreathed, oozing meats
as if they were jewels proposed for a noble's inspection.
He had lived ten years in New York
and as he spoke of this I saw there was a sadness
in him, but I couldn't tell whether it was the sadness
of something lost, or of something
not attempted. We were not interested in food
and ordered without flair;

and I saw this disappointed him and was sorry
but did nothing about it; we ourselves

were sad and nearly hysterical, bitter
over the loss of our love, and we ate
without speaking. I watched the man
sitting at a small table in the corner
folding napkins, and the expressions
that passed over his face — of grief, of anger and envy —
seemed to have lives of their own,
as if they only used the flesh of him
for passage, like pilgrims stepping from stone to stone,
crossing a river. For a second I almost saw
the way we are all related
as vessels or means for whatever it is
that charges through this world,
and I started to say I
almost could say, but my friend
tapped my hand and told me to pay the bill,
and I got up and followed him out
into the feckless sorrow and stupidity,
into the blazeless, empty day.

NEITHER ORNAMENTAL NOR TRUE

You say incredible things, like a gun
firing into the darkness — red, robust, unexpectedly
large flashes snapped
alive in the blackness, or you are lying out all night
in the garden, feeling your way among tomatoes and black-eyed peas,
turning the soil in your hands. Some things go to seed
no matter what you do. Which means, if you are a gardener,
the flowers come out, yellow
as coins on the turnip greens, white
on the peas, orange
on squash. You have become so dreamlike
to me, I can't remember who you once were. Are you the woman
who met the train in Kansas, and we rode out
until there were a hundred miles of wheat
in every direction, and black sky
we pulled like a blanket
over our bodies? Was that you? In the Midwest they say,
What I know *anymore*. Anymore
what I know
is you came to me shining
out of the dark day and mystery of the world
and I am leaving you there,
where I didn't find you.

FUCHSIA

Apprentice morning come easily now,
silver with fog and the breakdowns
of neighbors: shouts from up hill
where the land curls under vines and under the porches
of oaks, where even now
wintergreen and inkberry shiver forth
streamers of new growth, and the green frogs
suck at the dew and sing their bent songs.

It is easy
to hear my own voice in the liquid
contraltos of rage, the vents
and accusations that feed fires
up the hill. It is all human enough,
the yelling, capacious
and frank, the doors slamming, cries
of betrayal. I too have betrayed,
lost my place among the condensations
of commitment, dallied.
                  I go among friends
who say with neither fear nor fury in their voices
that they too don't know what's next, that from the studied
impactment of their lives
they have sallied small lines
of proposition, made a few calls. Slight affairs
shiver and fail; we go for a walk
by the rotunda, where, on the perishable lawn,
a band plays Dixieland — speaking,
not earnestly, but with steady intent,
of the play of choices, the simple chance
of another future somewhere else, perhaps a house
in the hills above L.A., part-time work
for the screen, a few avocado trees. For a while

it is as if the hazy play of evening light,
the splashes of music, the unbundled oaks
surrounding the Square, are enough
in themselves to sustain, as if mood
is itself sustenance, that our struggle to conceive
a continuance is of no more moment
than the fuchsia and soft yellow clothes of the tourists.

Perhaps it is possible
to be gentle no matter what, to seek not restraint
but surrender entirely, to turn
from the snarling reproach not into the keening
dismissal of hope but to whatever bright
fluttering is next, the bright fluttering
of wisteria petals, a felicitous
phrase, fingers touching
a face. How else to avoid
redemption,
or its opposite, which we stopped believing
in one day in high school, suddenly startled
over a steaming lunch tray by the way the fizzed
flowers of a stunted mimosa
seemed to beg for release? We realized then
we could say whatever we wanted, that the world
was no more particular
than anything else, it too could be out-argued,
confused by refusal or lies, that it was no wonder
people were stunned
by the eloquent permanence of death.
                                          So there is

permission, not granted
but given, as a forsythia at the edge of the walk,
having stolen more light

than it can contain, trembles, and the echoes
of argument fade into a fluttering
over the price of butterscotch floats,
and we are dazzled
by the gouge of perception, as if there was in fact a word
we were waiting to hear, not
as completion but as synoptic
and inevitable entitlement — the drift
of some stranger's conversation,
the memory of a thin mist
moored temporarily over the garden, that face
we saw from the window on the way to St. Albans: beautiful,
indifferent, unequivocably doomed.

CROOKED

I keep hanging to the fence outside
this garden watching sparrows primp
and bluster among the green profuse
bushes. I didn't know they sang,
hardly knew they were as social as
they are, little lumps exuberantly toss-
ing scraps under the bleeding hearts
and the hyacinths. In Carolina,
where I walked in a garden weekdays,
a man nagged me to take over his
plot, he pressed tomatoes and yellow
squash into my hands, and proposed
a calling of new tilled ground and
earthbound sweat. I was up to some-
thing else and wouldn't go along.
Birds squabbled there too, crows
and mockingbirds, waves of cedar
waxwings wheeling down all at once.
The man was small and too upset;
I heard later he had a stroke and
his daughters came and put him in
a nursing home where he sits in a
rolling chair with his head thrown
back, his mouth gaped, aware of
nothing. Sometimes I dream my ex-
wife has taken me back and we hoe
together a muddy row in some spring
garden. It's late afternoon, and,
for some reason, it's the nineteenth
century — buckboards, hand-cranked
cotton gins and the lot, the news-
paper set in wooden type. Her light
skirts are muddy and we are tired,

the sun is going down and we want
to quit, but then a crooked singing
of birds stirs from the woods and
we decide to go on a little longer.

FORTUNE

At a small monastery — or what had been
a monastery — outside Obrégon, we stopped;
you were suffering the hollow nausea of your first
pregnancy, sleeping as best you could
through the thousand miles of pines
and rocky fields of northern Mexico, so I went ahead
through the saddle-colored rooms, past
the broken church and the row of empty sheds,
where Indian women, according to a sign,
once baked the flat bread called *sapatos de Maria,*
to a garden in the back, over the parapet of which
I could see the river through some willows: a rinsed
bed of sand, dry now in winter.
                                        I didn't want a child,
and I was tired of closeness, tired
of being kind, so was glad to be alone
a while and lay down under a jacaranda tree,
and watched through leaves the changing pattern
of the sky, which I was tired of too, the scaly, stratospheric
winter clouds, edged with light, like the tiny waves
you pointed out, reflected on the bottom of a bridge
we rowed under in a rented boat, the day you told me
of the child — I was tired and slept.

It was nearly evening when I woke, two mestizo women
hurried talking through the tulip beds, the sky was pale.
They'd set small plaques among the plants,
naming them, the ornamentals and the fruit. Some,
so the writing said, were descendants
of the cuttings brought from Spain by monks;
intermingled here — Pinot grape with ocotillo,
damascena rose — they thrived. I thought of certain
tenderness, and forbearance, a man might bring

to vines and simple vegetables, cultivated
in memory of his home perhaps, in a foreign place;
and thought how sometimes what passes on from us
has little to do with what we hoped, but nonetheless
carries word of who we were and what we found.
For a moment then, among the arbors and the flower beds,
I did not feel so distant from this time and place,
and the edge of my own local fears began to dull.
I plucked a sprig — a leaf was all —
from a holly bush, and brought it out to you,
a little stronger in a portion of myself, a little
reconciled, though I couldn't know then
that in a month we would lose the child,
and in time you would pass,
like a squandered fortune, from my life.

CONFEDERATE STATES

It is so simple: our domesticated life
of tea and speculation, the armature of the trees
ample and contained outside the windows. We dream of Georgia,
of Michigan and Paris,
and go nowhere. This morning
        our bodies
might have saved us, but they didn't, charged
with nothing but physical contortion, a petty
fervor soon waning. We read books
and talk, assessing this, assessing that.
I have become more careful
than I ever thought possible, suited to an arrangement
which I don't defy. Why don't
        we light a fire in the middle of the room?
Why don't we sell bits of colored glass
at the beach? I am tired
and almost happy, though still I want to throw my life away,
some way I can't remember. The wind climbs furiously
in the oaks, but it is only wind,
no voice or metaphor for anything else. It is
        an adjustment, they say,
marriage, these orderly days, card games
and later supper, radishes carved to crowns. Brevet husband,
        I picture myself at twelve
sitting by the clear river I was raised on,
dragging a stick to attract bream. Trees
        stood in the water
and I imagined them drowning, the water
heaved upward through the muscle of pine,
choking resin, seeping into the spines of the needles —
        nothing else to do but fall.

IN VIRGINIA

I stalled a while watching a bay horse
crop grass in a small lot
near the highway. Blue spidergrass
and bitterweed flourished among piles
of rusted implements, among a hay rake with tines
like the delicate rib bones of an ancient fish, and old lumber.
I thought, the way one can, that the new loss
of your love
might become a permanent sadness,
and was sad
because I knew it wouldn't. We had not lingered
one evening in Virginia
to watch a bay mare, her coat roughed
already for winter, crop the sparse Bahia grass
in a cluttered lot — so it wasn't memory
that touched my sadness, though
what amplified the loss
was ample enough. And it wasn't
what might have been,
because I couldn't picture you
in that place, where a sly breeze
pretended to steal the smallest leaves, and the horse,
I saw, was old, and lame. We imagined children
and hard work, waking by the lake
in Michigan, but we got
to none of these. I read a passage once
about a form of chastity
that acknowledged,
but abstained from pursuing,
the beauty of the world, and I thought of the afternoon
I turned to you on the beach at Pamet Roads
and saw your face for an instant
shining like all I would ever love

or had ever loved, and though the moment passed
like one of the thin green waves
skittering in, I knew
I had already given myself away,
that I would make the mistake
I had made before,
and would probably make again, of believing
your face, your voice, your
history, would knot my life
to itself,
and so wind up lost. They say it isn't the squalor
that kills, it's the beauty. It's what — and all —
on a bright day
when as we watch the light tremble in sheets
on the pond, we surrender to,
and so go dumbly down,
and are ruined,
and return from dazed and chastened,
as a callow boy caught thieving in an orchard
will glance at the bootless blue sky,
at the treasure of ripe fruit
filling his shirt, and descend
into the irate farmer's world,
unable to explain anything —
not his theft, or himself,
or what makes him what he is.

TRANSFORMATION TO WHITE

Some stranger's
clever, coincidental conversation
is preparing me
for solitude; it rises and fades
as I step onto the avenue where just down there
trees shaped like the entrances to caves
are barring the light from this side of Manhattan.
Sometimes I want to pass completely

unnoticed through my life, I want to become
like the melted light
pouring down on the roofs of cars, filling
the street and the windows,
then fading. In a minute

I will pause under the fruit-choked trees
bandaging a derelict house on Eleventh
to speak a small sermon
on the redundancies of joy.
I believe, though crushed and
randomly derelict, we might yet
thrust our hands into abundance
& be provisioned. Darkness has slipped out

among us, and the first lightning bugs of summer,
blinking over the miniature gardens of Manhattan, tremble
and sway. I could tell you I am tired
of marriage, of ambition,
and effort, but who isn't, and how
would that explain my survival
and make its triumph touch you? Nearby new apartments
go up in something called the Memphis style;
they are salmon colored with curved, snapped-on

balconies, harmoniously
advertised, but no one happy with his life
would live there, no one would want
to pass from this world
through the Sheetrock surfaces and pale
hallways of the Memphis
style. Tonight I will pay seven

dollars to see a woman sit before me
naked, and I am glad I live in a world where a woman
will do this, so simply, making
small talk as she strokes her shaved cunt.
Her breasts are fragile, as soft
as the skin of a baby: the relic,
unveiled flesh through which we might touch
the perfection
we once were. But this thought too
I cast aside, uneasy
with its effortless and dated
resolution. It isn't childhood I'm
looking for from the women
clustered near the piers — it's something older, and worse.
    Nonetheless,

sated with the spill of jism, I will be
satisfied, momentarily relieved
again; I will thank her
honestly, and a smile will slide out between us,
not the smile of those who hope for twinship,
or for the union of congruent souls,
but of those for whom the paying of debts,
the unpretentious carrying through
of a simple exchange,

has become enough. As I come
she will be speaking of a beach in Florida
she visited with her husband. She will say
it was sunset when they knelt by the water
and touched each other's face
with salt. "I could see the moon
shining on us," she will say. "It was the color of pearls,
and it turned us, and everything near us, white."
Maybe I will hear her voice

later as I grope toward sleep. Maybe, as the body
of my wife turns once more,
so that I feel brushing my back
the shape of the flesh I know best in the world,
maybe I will hear, as I did for a moment then,
the simplified eloquence
of a humanness
so apparent, so undistilled,
that I cannot resist it.

KOHAKU

The first time we made love
we crawled away from your brother's campfire
on Carabelle Beach and lay down under a thin blanket
among the burnt pine stumps. You were thirteen
and I was sixteen, younger
than any lovers we ever knew
in the world. For years I thought I had ruined you.
Even after we married
and later divorced and both of us had gone on
to two more marriages apiece, I thought
I had taken something from you that night
and all the other nights, when we lay down in cornfields,
in the bitter yellow grasses by the road,
in your aunt's sun-dusty attic bedroom — and your body,
so pale it seemed sometimes almost transparent,
turned to me, came harshly
against me as if ridden by a will of its own — even then
I thought I had stripped you of choice
in some way, taken only out of selfishness
and desire. I suppose that's my own
lookout now and is only a dry question
from the past that can go without answering.
We broke up, went into the world, grew desperate,
found each other again and, in a rush
of affection and relief, married. We moved
to the mountains, to a white house set into a notch
above a shallow stream. I fished for trout, picked
apples with the local orchard-men; you taught
school. In the evening we walked across the steep pasture
I helped the landlord clear of rocks on Saturdays.
I remember turning over a stone
the size and shape of a loaf of bread to find a black
widow spider underneath. Its ruby helix

41

shone like a jewel
from some lost kingdom. It was so beautiful
I wanted to give it to you,
but I crushed it under my boot instead.
In the winter,
as ice inched out into the stream, you grew nervous
and I grew sullen. We took sudden,
hair-raising trips to Philadelphia
and the Yucatan. In spring
we planted a garden, lost
it to beetles. You made flowers
out of red paper that you set like lanterns
in the cedar trees. From the porch at night
I would watch them, their color faded white
and ghostly, shivering and bobbing
in the breeze, and think of Japan,
of intimacy and flight. Rain washed them out,
but you made others. Toward the end of May
I thought I was turning into you; I would wake at night
to touch breasts and the long, polished
legs, the brief pubis,
imagining, maybe becoming, maybe being,
the frightened and dumbfounded
inhabiter of your body. My mouth formed words,
but it was you who spoke, you
who turned with flour to your elbows, a streak
of white curving across your forehead, you
who stood in the wind
calling our dog with names
that didn't belong to him, or to me.

RENEWAL: A VERSION

I rise to the dismissive woods, tangle of catbrier
like a new language teaching itself to trees, the potholes,
trickling stream,
                and though I am whizzing
with terror — lost, bamboozled — it is no time before
I come to the sea edge, the remarkable boundary fashioned
                            of weeds
and mud, see beyond a headland of dunes the ship masts,
the delicate rigging.
                There are boys swimming a race
                        between boats;
there is war debris, and broken palms; there is a sky of
                         silk,
hibiscus, bananas in piles.

                I don't know where the morning
                has gone,
but I know I am in a different country; I lean against a
                thatched shed
eating guava and lime, I discuss a Victorian procedure
with a large man in blue spats, I claim to be celibate,
I own a house with a verandah, my mother is lame. I think
                you should see

the afternoon here, I think you should lie in a hammock
and watch the day take the bandage from its back
because already from the vise of the moon falls star salt,
and the marsh grass is golden and blowing in breeze, and
                someone is counting to ten

in a language in which the vowels are so voluptuous
and tender you think you might weep, and the sexes have
                mingled

to the point they are almost interchangeable, and they say
                                          the mayor
is leaving office to become a priest, he has carried
                                          his belongings

already into the ruins of the temple (you can see him there,
in early morning when the sun is white as the stones, wearing
a red shawl and chanting his prayers) — and small boys herd
                                          dogs like sheep,
and we all wear flowers now,
and we don't live on memory or hope, or excursions
of blame, and though I don't know how I got here,
and though I am lying, I have opened a shop to sell
certain small trinkets — jujubes and relics — and I have let
the fingernails of my right hand grow long and painted my
                                          belly blue

and I have taken a wife who is slender and black as the night
and she sings to me, oh, she sings to me . . .

THREE

RAISON D'ÊTRE

Singed, rent, or whatever,
the dirty boys bait their hooks
with bugs,
which are bitter and stink and won't make fish
rise, either today
or tomorrow — or tomorrow when the green
gloves of spring once more begin
to strangle the city, and old women
pour onto the avenues
for confabulation and argument,
becoming proof of God's
existence in this part of the world, which for a moment,
as a small boy draws back the striped plastic pole,
becomes a song of tenderness,
like a hot night on the sixth floor
when, above the stinks and
cries, your sister
reaches across the milky light
to fan you for a minute, just a minute,
though she doesn't really mean it,
or she doesn't do it long enough
for you — or her — to know
if she means it; but that moment
is like a peach somebody hands you
in a battle trench, or like the door
you opened once, where you shouldn't have been,
to see a beautiful woman
slipping into a silver sequined dress . . .

The arms draw back, the reel
flashes in the sun, it is spring. If you see
them tonight you will not know at whom you look,
these scarred boys whose love

of life is incidental, like the wind
that leaps the railing to furiously shake, for a second,
the tops of a few sycamores, and whose
fear of death
is nonexistent; all they know
and remember
has become performance,
a tinny, sharp routine
danced for quarters, their hands dark
from the blood of fishes, their eyes shining.

AFTER THE GAME

Our drunk buddy shuffles past the grandstand
and falls on his face in the grass.
We don't know what's wrong with him
so pick him up, laughing at his foolishness,
but he will have none
of our help: solitary, independent,
stern as a goalpost, he stares us back
into our postgame celebration, pulls
the silver whiskey from his pocket
and takes a drink. We have just leapt
with sixty thousand others to our feet
as the team trampled its way into the visitors' end zone
and are hearty now, reassured
that our shaky lives
can still find a moment's merit,
and so do not want to support such obvious delapidation
as our friend represents, is. But he begins to rail at us,
accusing us of all manner of falsehood, consistent
for a moment in execration and sorrow,
a tall man with a face out of control, rapacious
and mad, demanding what we don't have: some solace
that he missed years ago
on the front steps of his life. He says we are liars,
he reminds us that we don't really love our wives,
that our children are vicious
and vacuous; there is an earnestness, a trembling
fire that compels him, but we
who have already been lifted up
by the gouge and stab of frenzy — by the game —
do not need, cannot use,
what he demands we accept. We josh,

we thump his back and drag him onward,
jolly as the heroes of Troy
with the clanging blue Mediterranean
still years from devouring us.

RITES

As the boy buckling
himself into the harness of a gull-wing
sail looks down
at the arrested green flow of mountain valleys,
where even now cloud shadow
pulls for Tennessee, and the sky —
tilted toward the north
so the heaviest colors (scarlet lead,
yellow iron) slide down —
becomes abstract,
                he thinks of himself
as magisterial
& recumbent, picturing
the white walls of a prison
receding like the white tear
of sea foam polished into blue;
                     and runs
the six steps to the cliff's edge
& leaps

to find the air not a highway
but the complicated froth
and bluster of a larger body
than any he has ever known — pumping
and heaving
& whistling
a tune
about higher — higher —
fly higher —

thus our descent begins.

SONNET

At the track
my father said *Bet this horse,*
and I gave him all my money
& lost
and wouldn't forgive him.
Now he sits at dawn on the other bed
offering grandiose schemes
to charm my love back. I hear the wind
stumbling in the sea oats,
the cries of purple martins diving at the sea.
The light is dim
and gray, hardly touched by morning.
My father's hands are gross
with age and the residue
of strength. I have seen him lean his back
against an upright wedged and half-sawn pine
to make it fall
where he wanted. I cannot pretend
to be asleep. I do not know
whether love can save me.

TOO MUCH, NEVER ENOUGH

Snow patches on the sea dunes
make my brother remember the desert. He saw
white rocks there, and rocks
the color of wheat. Everything, he says,
in the desert looked abandoned, hundred-year-old
wheel ruts — true as rails — slinking on
permanently. As if even the air
had vanished, he says. I know my brother
can't get enough
of the barren, eroded places, and I think how curious
it is that in a world so voluptuous
we have to squint our eyes
to keep from being redeemed by its beauty,
he must press the valances of his own heart
until, like an abused child, it squats in a corner,
seeking nothing. Under the bridge
the tidal river sucks at grasses, and the sweet stink of sea life
is all around us; a green and white skiff
perches on a backyard rack, and the pond beneath the hill
is oiled to a shine so brilliant
it hurts the eyes. I say this,
and he says yes that's it — it hurts
the eyes. In a straw hat
he found by a road in Nogales
he leans his head against the window
and closes his eyes against light
and the teetering breath of the world, conjuring,
against odds, a life simple
as rock, something treeless
and obsolete, the figment of a parched god, —
one hopeless and disfigured,
who understands creation as erasure,
as a pure act of limitation,

offered
neither as adornment
or supplication —
to himself, or itself — that holiness
is bleak,
even existence
a sin.

NUMBER SIX SHOT

The black dog swims strongly,
breaking ice as he goes, smashing
the dead lilies and the sticks of grass,
heaving, as if he would come out of his body,
toward the dying mallard, which he will
find in a moment, cradled
in a patch of maidencane, its breast shattered
by Number Six Remington shot, its black eye
open under the black softness of the small lid,
its black beak half-open. As we rise
in the frail bateau,
having come this long way across early dark
into the private world
of a choked and drowning pond
on the edge of Wisconsin, where just now
the sky sags under the weight of blue battered
clouds, and winter is a claim
about to be made, the story you
told about shooting your father
to death twenty years ago,
on just such a hunt as this,
begins to insinuate itself
into the heart of things, so that for ten seconds
I forget the strong dog
and look at your face which has been
hard for a long time now, maybe twenty years,
and I don't even try
to tell you anything about
how difficult life is,
or about how there must be a
reason — I just snap another shell
into the chamber,
and whistle the dog left

toward the bird he can't see but will find soon,
and plunge my free hand
into the black water,
up to the elbow,
as if I might grope the stopper in my fingers
to drain away the whole scene,
or casually draw up for you to see
some ancient trinket still glittering,
so you might, for a moment, be appeased.

AS IN JAPAN THIS MORNING

Somehow I have come close
to the intractable mind
obsessed with a woman's foot
in a pleasant white sandal,
with a glance
that lifts from a stream
through a small village
and its sheltering pines
to the sharp green edges
of a mountain range. The wind lives
in the objects it manipulates,
not apart. May I say
an old man told me this?
Only necessity compels,
but what, after all,
is necessary? The old warrior
sits at his window
attempting to concentrate, says, *Snow
is a white wing* — holds that:
not the object,
but the act. After a while
it is simply too much.
He is walking through an orange grove,
driving a small cart
downhill breakneck,
arguing with a woman: pictures hurtling by.
Faith is simply the memory
of the swift passage stopped.
It doesn't matter on what:
a bundle of cedar shingles,
a lamp across the river
in a house you thought abandoned —
often it is light

or an equivalent — ;
as in Japan this morning,
the old warrior's glance
catches on the bright dew buds
glittering on a red scarf
forgotten on a wash line,
and rests there a moment
before plunging helplessly on.

OKEFENOKEE STELLAE

So we must build to the moment
when the doe and her fawn step
from the cedars and walk carefully
across the matted field to the pond.

                                        This is in the swamp

and is not seen from tower or trail,
from the immaculate boardwalk
laid like hydrofoil
amidst myrtle and neverwet

and bayberry bush, tending
sinuously in a horizontal
falling away, to bring us — explorers —
to the prairie edge, where hammocks of cypress

sail like galleons on an ocean of reeds. We must rise
like tourists
on firm steps of emotion, of penetration, as the body
penetrates the late afternoon breeze, and a construction,

as if, walking, or climbing the observation tower,
we are making a road,
as a dream or myth will flatten the landscape before us,
unrolling an avenue of reddened pavement

and hyacinths in ditches . . .

                              — which is to say
we must mention we have arrived here alone,
that lover or friend is lost

somewhere behind us, that no matter
how we hoodoo

or preen, it is still an unusual
world, one in which the hawk

rises on her singular column of air,
winding the spiral
that moment to moment becomes more abstract —
though occasionally sun-

shined and almost transfiguring,
if we think of stillness amidst motion —
so attach ourselves
or penetrate, not idea,

but perception, as if life — this having come to us —
were not mastery or endurance,
but integration, or simply
a dissolution entirely

of self into object,
which at the moment is not even object
but the path made of boards — seen from the tower now —
raveled behind, the tall, broad-belled

cypress like those geese
stretching their necks on a pond down home,
signifying
only what we are inclined

to receive, be it perpetuation
of loneliness, the harmonics articulate
in the sallow silk light, the cry of an owl
with its four descents

of abandonment, or the moment
when as the day slides back into the sheath of woods
a doe and her fawn
step forth,

and with the cautious elegance
of those for whom life includes
the possibility of murder,
approach the pond — it shimmers

with cold dark light — and carefully drink.

THE DEFIANCE OF HEROES

In stories the old hero turns from the house
to linger in the courtyard
staring up long at the stars.
The scent of green wheat drifts from the fields,
tinged with the scent of the sea. In the stars
he sees the mouths of women and strong arms
raised. He can almost remember
what it felt like
to hold the golden bundle in his hands,
to raise it in the polished light
so high
the sun blazed brighter; and the stiff seas,
already legendary,
each wave an illuminated page
in his life's heraldry,
revealing another green island;
and the violence, free of rage
and lust — a pure, clear stream,
his whole body the stream.

Now, in another kingdom,
he sighs,
but not over loss, the fantastic adventuring.
Though goats bleating in the pen, the old stone house,
parched fields and contentious family are pitiful,
they do not matter. They do not matter.
Voyages end only
to reveal the ample treasure:

there is no home in this world.

NOT YET

The scrap of pink net filled
with fish fat and seeds
is gone from the willow tree,
and the birds are on their own,
free now to come up with the spirignum
necessary to make it in the woods.
Juncoes and peewits, vireos
and sparrows must fall back now
on their own resources, toughen
and take responsibility. Some won't make it.
Some have gotten used to the free lunch,
dependent, hooked
on someone else's hard work
to save them. And it's too bad
the way spring plays with us this year,
waving a bright handkerchief
out winter's window, laughing
with an irrepressible glee
we continue to hear,
like a sweet echo, for quite some time
after the shutters have been pulled
and we are left to the harsh bellowing
of the wounded Achillean cold.

AMERICAN DRIFT

i.

I remember father stooping
to haul my drunken mother from the pond.
His careful, ambiguous caresses
that did not relieve her, or us. What do you do
in a life where courage fails? My brother
drives stocks
on the dirt track circuit. When he crashes
the body of the car flies apart.
I saw him sitting, humped in the frame,
unhurt, as behind the chicken-wire fence
spectators stared in silence. Life
is so disastrous and difficult
you can't blame anyone
for throwing it away.
There are not enough pleasures
to simplify the spirit.

ii.

I got down on my knees
and planted radishes. Kept
a daily garden-diary: the slim shoot,
rising bent, splits within a morning
into two leaves, heart-shaped,
and goes from there.

Flowers on the beans
the size and shape of salmon scales.
Wisp of tarragon. Dank monstrosity
of melon.

Only in memory I sought rebirth.
At the time I walked mornings among the butter beans
I'd dusted flour on to keep deer away,
cursing the coons whose withered, old-men's feet
and bitter scut polluted order.

iii.

Stubbornly,
love persists. I can't understand
how it is so tough
and persevering. I cannot live
if I cannot give to you. And to you.

Carillon at dusk. Light
fading out over water. In the park
at Chamonix we watched the trout
gliding under fallen linden leaves.
It seemed perpetual. Is there such,
inevitable and sustaining? A field
of blueberries, swollen ripe,
unpicked, on the slope of Mount Nicolas.

My brother died insane. Mother's
liver burst. Father found no courage.
America is slipping through my fingers.
I am sick of this country,
sick of hope. I can't blame anyone for giving up.
I can't blame anyone for setting off alone.

FOUR

RIDING IN WATER

My memories are common, memories of baseballs
asleep all night in the blackened pocket
of a Spalding glove, of red enamel
peppers heaped on a green table, of the wind nagging
the line of sycamores along my father's drive —
but tonight, alone in this sea
town, I think only of the time my best friend and I
rode all the way across Apalachee Bay, lowered
and laid into the green bow wave of his brother's boat, our free hands
just touching through the spilled phosphorous
pushed up in careful passage over the evening waters. I suppose
the lights of the beach houses appeared
among the pines like white birds
settling in for the night. I suppose we believed
we rode the best moment of our lives;
   — I remember the few words
we spoke as our forked sleek and brown bodies
dragged above the seabed
where the green grasses called *mermaids' hair*
bent flowing, conjured
toward sleep by the gentle and relentless hand
of the tide. We said *yes, yes,* speaking the names of girls
with the reverence of penitents, swearing,
as if our future lay relaxed and permanent
in the seas of the moon, that we would love them
forever, which we have. We saw the stars
take their places, orchestral
and perfected, and I suppose as we looked southward
past the island where our families, drugged
by the sea days, sprawled on the porch
fashioning charitable stories
from the gaudy breeze
riding in under the wing of Florida night — I suppose

we did not mind or harken
the stiff seas bristling
beyond, as if, in the commonness
of time, there was a moment
we understood without acknowledging
when the dangerous world
was simply a white line of wave crest
that the night would erase.

TESTAMENT OF WHITE, PART TWO: THE PAST

On the Georgia island where I was raised
you can walk two miles down a strand
that wasn't there when I was a boy. Crows
pick at the fresh range of sea trash, and dogs,
set loose from tourist trucks, bound oblivious
and larking down the beach. From the new Point,
where the waves touch the pale sand with a tenderness
that is almost tenderness, that is almost
the same slow and fragile caress
as my tongue licking across your breasts,
you can look back across two miles of brand-new emptiness —
perhaps not emptiness, perhaps only the world unfilled yet — and see
among the green anarchic dunes one or two
that look like the roofs of houses; and if you have come there,
alone or with someone, in that disorderly muted time of day
when the ocean and the sky
appear as two versions of the same simplified
and transient color: teal-gray, seal-blue,
incandescent evening, you might imagine you saw lights
shining under those eaves that are not eaves,
and imagine lives lived there: a woman
calling husband and child to supper,
the three of them sitting down at a small wiped table,
tasting in their nostrils the odors of bread
and boiled greens, their hands
moving through and within the light
as they pass plates and bowls; and, if you are needful,
you might imagine this scene as complete
and continuing, the harmonics perfected,
as the light shining forth from windows is perfected,
and the thick walls of the house,
and the rowed dunes behind — which are slipping

uncontrollably into their shadows —
and the shadows stitching together the night,
and all you have dreamed and hoped for
on this earth that is vanishing.

PERCEPTION TWO

The world this morning is no miracle
facsimile; it is the large wind
off the sea squealing and punching at the town, pools
collecting around the drains, and workmen, those who
must go out no matter what, vivid in yellow slicks,
arguing a point of romance and abandonment
as they enter the store for coffee.
                                    Sometimes, say this morning,
the car won't start and I sit there with the rain muddling
the windshield and think of a dream where we caught fish all night,
fish that made glittering cartwheels on the surface
as we hauled them overhand, and then perhaps,
as the rain scuffs the hedges, I think of a woman I loved
and let go and how my life might be different . . .
                                            I wished
for a sense of purpose, a righteousness
that was clear and naturally translated
into action; a movement without thought, a release of the self . . .

For days now the thought of journeys
has estranged me from the place I live; the spindly
water tower and the uphill road leading
through a maple thicket to the train station —
converted now to shops selling curios
and posters of rock and roll stars — the one poolroom
with its collection of beer signs like altars of neon,
the spatterings of yellow paint on the sidewalk
before the Knights of Columbus hall — all, that is to say,
including perhaps even the various pasts
carelessly arranged in the minds of my friends, have been investigated
already, marked, as on a field day, by small blue flags indicating
distance — of sorrow, exuberance, dilation . . . — and cannot

become more again
than they are.
                    On summer nights
I listened to band music drifting from the Square,
and the sad articulation of its amateur earnestness
seemed chastened to me, informing me on those evenings
when the streetlights tangled in trees, of a pure
continuing aggression, the consanguineous twitch
that, though soothed for a moment as the overhead wires,
light-caught, turned into silver,
argued a more rigorous and permanent detachment, a bitter seam
at the joining of desire and effort — and so, for a time,
I stood aside, as one called away by a stranger
who holds in his hand something glittering meanly,
but bright
and offered to us . . .
                    So I took long walks,
attended family reunions, listened all afternoon to a cousin
describe the death of his son, spoke of bitterness and failure,
the transparent defiance of a child, mutual
funds; I was seeking
perhaps only a momentary inflection, a hand casual
and temperate touching my hair — once, it seemed,
after splintering, indeterminate rain, the day might blaze up,
and the sun scratching the water, refractive and distant beyond the
     tidal flats,
seemed particular in its harmonies, transubstantial
and coaslescent, as if the purpose of all things
might any moment become apparent, and, despite myself,
I was charged with exhilaration
that promised to propel me
beyond any bias or fragmentary prejudice, and turned

to my neighbor to tell him,
but found myself alone.

It is still early;
the world
under rain that heaves and jostles,
attempting to prove, like a neglected child
whacking trees and the side of the house all morning,
that something must be attended to, is whittled
and frail — or so it must be
in the transference of memory and knowledge, the slow
gathering of intention that may not be intention
but only the summary weight
of a life in itself; as the mind drifts
in the rhythm of wipers thwacking the bodice
and the one I have stayed with this time longer than any other
turns to ask if I would like to go in for coffee,
a simplified peace, like a gathering of birds, comes on
independently,
and I am indistinguishable
from myself, preserved and saturated
by something as simple as breath, and as dire,
though I do not understand this, and cannot hold it,
or use it perhaps, live in it briefly,
and try to remember, and go on, forgetting.

CYCLES

I think it is well known now
how you can take one part of the country
and re-erect it somewhere else, how the abrupt, snow-streaked
mountains of New Mexico hang in a dark corner
of your uncle's hall. And some morning in late winter
the trees are diadems of ice,
the way they were once, miraculously, on the river in Florida,
when you were a child. It is not
that we wish the courage
to ask a co-worker
for the loan of her beach house, it is not
that. Or the madwoman,
slick with terror and grease, interrupting mass —
that something in here
would take hold suddenly, and calm her. O the priests
do their duty
because they are pros. And the world
was always crumbling fast; it is not that we wish the world
other than it is. My friend asks
what's your hurry? we are all headed
to the grave. Only, I guess,
I seek a certain rhythm, the dumb bob
of a pigeon's head, the old friend
calling from Kansas, the muck of love —
its resignation and exuberance — the red flowers
returned to the trees
as if winter was nothing to them, nothing at all.

ROMANCE

My wife and I make love in the hot
roll-away bed, careful for most of it because
we think it's a good idea in the heat
not to touch, but then my arms give
way and I let myself down onto her feverish
body, and the sweat springs out.
We are like two cumbersome
alligators, or the couple
I can't stop thinking of, whose car
flipped into the river and sank
into four feet of mud,
upside down and crushed, so that when they
finally winched them out and hauled
them to the morgue they had to scrape
mud off their open eyeballs. I keep hoping someone,

at that moment when their dead sight
cleared again, remembered
a little tenderness, maybe found a little something
in his heart, a recognition
of how this might happen to any
of us, how no matter the weather
or the dark we might reach
anyway for an embrace, we might
say something foolish
and loving and scrape the back
of our hand across somebody's
shoulder dumbly,
here in the sloppy day, as we
try for one second

to get past our ignorance,
to forget the stupid bird-
song and the traffic and what's haywire
and always will be.

NOW I SMACK MY HEAD

I've taken too many things seriously,
for example: that there is inherent
seriousness in everything,
if we can just locate it, it being
our duty to try. Now I smack my head
and cry *How could I have been so stupid —*
the rain is only the rain, my
boy. But then I am coming out of the library, late,
after watching Laurel and Hardy
in *Sons of the Desert,* and already I can't stop
thinking of Oliver Hardy's face,
the four thousand expressions, from horror
to smirkery, that pass over it
as he waits for his wife
to let him have it, and rain is dripping
from the aged ginkgo dumbly springing its leaves
again, there is the smell
of pizza dough, a wet dog crosses the street,
and I can't do anything
for about ten seconds but stand there
with my heart pounding wildly,
seriously in love with it all.

GOSNOLD POND

I.

I get everything I can
from the woods, and from the black ice-pond
where the ice for some reason I can't exactly
figure is stippled and rutted, as if just as it
froze in the empty night without a soul
stirring, it shuddered, flung
itself feebly against the cold, and fell back. I mean here

is a gang of depressions where the water sucked down around grass
    stems,

where now, trapped in starry rays, brown
bits of furze, the shape and color

of woolly caterpillars

hang suspended; and the grass stems are snapped
at the point they stick from the ice, and
have been swept away, stems and dry flower heads — gathered
by the wind and blown off to stuff the bedding
of the woods. This is all today perambulating

under a sky rich with reds and sallow orange, a day
when the wind throbs in the trees, making
a crumpling sound which is not the sound of crumpling branches

but a sound as if the wind itself were crumpling.

II.

The flock of black birds rising
makes a sound of sewing machines; the birds rise

above the low, bare snow-capped hills
and disappear toward the west, as, out on the ice,
walking carefully,
                    I think of the one

who spoke of the aura the earth has
when it remembers its lost beauty, and I cannot say
when that time was anymore, though I know what

we have done, I know about the shellfish dying on the shallow beds,

the poisoned birds, the raccoon convulsing, its black
monkey-hands gripping and gripping
on nothing — know about the flotsam,
the brassy cigarette pack embedded in the ice
ten miles from store or house, the single

unclasped shoe that I can see standing on the bottom,

particularly poignant
because it is a child's shoe, which means
it is more than lost, because, even if found,
the child will have grown out of it
into another life entirely. But I cannot say

this means much to me, nor
do I ask for indulgence as I shuffle
and slide to a stop on this pond, where I too,
in a sense, am standing on the bottom, since on a day

of zero degrees this is as far down
as one can go — but, and to return, I cannot say

the old world has abandoned me, that what was once beautiful

III.

has fled, because this all: the rachitic trees
that are mauve and ocher in the highest branches,
the brief slips of snow whispered into ridges
on the ice, the vivid red
of berries in the holly bushes, the cast-off, slight

rising birds are still an essential
and unremarkable enbrandishment of a vigorous
though changed life, and even debris
is not necessarily an intrusion, not the flimsy,
cracked skeleton of a squirrel under the evergreen
inkberry bush, nor the flakes of colored paper
cast down in pine straw,
                              nor the burn marks

like raised shovel blades
at the base of the oaks, for it is all
simply this day's gathering, the reaped

event and emplacement of time

and design — a man
standing in a gray winter coat
in the middle of a pond in Massachusetts only a single,
though not yet obsolete, participant —

so the possibility,
as in the western sky the day
burns itself clean, of night,

becomes night.

THE MEANING OF BIRDS

Of the genesis of birds we know nothing,
save the legend they are descended
from reptiles: flying, snap-jawed lizards
that have somehow taken to air. Better the story
that they were crab-apple blossoms
or such, blown along by the wind; time after time
finding themselves tossed from perhaps a seaside tree,
floated or lifted over the thin blue lazarine waves
until something in the snatch of color
began to flutter and rise. But what does it matter
anyway how they got up high
in the trees or over the rusty shoulders
of some mountain? There they are,
little figments,
animated — soaring. And if occasionally a tern washes up
greased and stiff, and sometimes a cardinal
or a mockingbird slams against the windshield
and your soul goes *oh God* and shivers
at the quick and unexpected end
to beauty, it is not news that we live in a world
where beauty is unexplainable
and suddenly ruined
and has its own routines. We are often far
from home in a dark town, and our griefs
are difficult to translate into a language
understood by others. We sense the downswing of time
and learn, having come of age, that the reluctant
concessions made in youth
are not sufficient to heat the cold drawn breath
of age. Perhaps temperance
was not enough, foresight or even wisdom
fallacious, not only in conception
but in the thin acts

themselves. So our lives are difficult,
and perhaps unpardonable, and the fey gauds
of youth have, as the old men told us they would,
faded. But still, it is morning again, this day.
In the flowering trees
the birds take up their indifferent, elegant cries.
Look around. Perhaps it isn't too late
to make a fool of yourself again. Perhaps it isn't too late
to flap your arms and cry out, to give
one more cracked rendition of your singular, aspirant song.

RESPITE

Someone walking in the Western dust
says *Our lives*
are not ours to take away,
and I am immensely relieved by this, I think
it means we can get on with whatever haphazard
project we've signed
on to do, whether it's my brother's
scheme to move the red sandstone
mountain off his homestead
in Utah, or that painter,
the aborigine I met three
years ago, who was the last one who knew
the ancient designs he painted from root
and jackflower dye onto bark,
and was so solemn and so solemnly
happy about it — happy the way we were happy,
making love all afternoon, as finally the rain
broke through the heat wave,
and we watched the ivy
on the next building gather the silver droplets,
and the shouts from the street
became muted,
almost tender, as above the city
lightning flashed
and the suicides climbed down from the roofs.

THE HOLLY TREE

More than a tragically impaired
sense of moral perception
is implied here as I watch the local householder
hack down the holly tree in his backyard. It is of course
the only domesticated holly for thirty miles, a shabby tree
with leaves that look waxed, a tree from which everything,
barring life itself,
has been expunged, but still a tree. Walking by I sneeze;
he says, *Salud*,
and again, *salud*. Perhaps this is consideration
he shows me, at least acknowledgment
of fellow humanness. I stop to ask him why he kills the tree
and listen to his story — which includes the arm of his son
broken from a fall, needle thorns scratching
his face, bird shit, his wife's hatred of the dull,
yellowish, evergreen leaves. Younger,
I would have energetically explained the special
consideration he owes the tree, its singularity
among the ragged seaside flora on this peninsula; perhaps,
I would say, it is the simple stitch
that holds darkness away; perhaps
it is connection or emblem, aggregate and
fulcrum of the interspiritual penetration
of omnipresence, immanent
revelation — by God, the Christ, the Son of Allah, Krishna himself.
What I say is, *Mind*
if I take a sprig?
which I do, and walk on down the descendant street
where beyond the peaked and gathered roofs

the fresh sea glitters, another
frail extravagance, I guess, depleted,
epicene and impermanent too.

THE RIVER

Finally I know who is traveling
with me, how every morning now I get up, and there are Willie
Mays and Raphael Soyer and Haystacks
Calhoun going on with their lives, and the rose

of Sharon bush, or some rose of Sharon,
blooms all summer, and will again next summer in the garden
at St. Lukes, which it looks like they won't tear
down for a taxi garage; it looks like

even the crab apples and forsythia,
which after all are perennials — they don't say this
about us — will continue, having stepped forth
to do their uncomplicated and slightly off-color
routines in the universal talent show; and that dab

of green paint, splashed near the brick bottom
of a house on Grove, will probably still be there
when my children's children
skip around the corner, balancing
fractions in their minds like spinning plates, new love
already grinding their small hearts, as, several

times, returning from school
along a route of probably not more than
four blocks — that's all it takes — they will observe
a profound number of articles and human
emotions, a short, ragged man possibly, explaining
his misery to a building, ripe peaches,
and those stains on the sidewalk,
worn to the shape of horses — that

is to say, the whole gaudy show
careening on not like a river
we sink into and float downstream on the back of —
there's no need — but a river we step into
and wade, swim fitfully,
and climb out of onto a shore that from here
looks like Crete or Portland, or some other place
we never dreamed we'd wind up in.

STAGE LIGHT

Up ahead, beyond a rising foreground that is going
green to umber, beyond the inconclusive screen

of barely feathered branches, riders stream
as silently as moths along the roadway

toward an amber streetlight. They look
as if they are riding into sunset, but it is the sun-

set of stage light, worn and fallow, soft
and compelling as the light in theatrical backyards,

those places where the failed father
walks after the last session with his broken son,

in which he has admitted, finally and too late,
that he betrayed him. From willows near the light

stream complex wisped branches that are as delicate
as the stems of flowers. The wind takes them

softly in soft hands, and sets them swaying,
like the childhood swing that continues to sway

in the empty backyard, after it is all over,
after the father, who does not know any more

now than before, but who has come at last to a disaster
he can't evade, does the next, last thing,

after we, in that brocaded moment
when the final action has already occurred —

but before the saving house-lights go up — lie collapsed
in exhaustion, in which we see

our own betrayal, that is not fearful
or overargued now, but complete,

and strangely comfortable. For a moment,
as the thin stars begin their explanation

of night, as the birds give up their crossed
cries — so abruptly, as if

a drape has fallen — I wonder about a fate, or
whatever it is that describes the linkage of a life

drawn tight and inevitable, that can
snatch a man up, like a father worn out by his stumbling,

and carry him; and I wonder if this could really happen
to us, and if our argument against, or defiance of this,

has no substance — or if it has,
if it is already too late — so that time, and what

we have learned, is preserved and carried forth,
is *provocative,* only as gesture — a snatch of song

dying on the water of the mind, the sunset dying
on a theater wall, the aged actor who, already in memory,

moves still, with the earnest collapsed delicacy
of the convicted, toward his death.

Printed in the United States
95206LV00002B/5/A

Made in the USA
San Bernardino, CA
11 July 2014